Facts About the Labrador Retriever

By Lisa Strattin

© 2019 Lisa Strattin

FREE BOOK

FREE FOR ALL SUBSCRIBERS

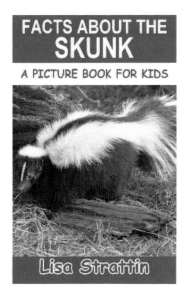

LisaStrattin.com/Subscribe-Here

BOX SET

- **FACTS ABOUT THE POISON DART FROGS**
- **FACTS ABOUT THE THREE TOED SLOTH**
- **FACTS ABOUT THE RED PANDA**
- **FACTS ABOUT THE SEAHORSE**
- **FACTS ABOUT THE PLATYPUS**
- **FACTS ABOUT THE REINDEER**
- **FACTS ABOUT THE PANTHER**
- **FACTS ABOUT THE SIBERIAN HUSKY**

LisaStrattin.com/BookBundle

Facts for Kids Picture Books by Lisa Strattin

Little Blue Penguin, Vol 92

Chipmunk, Vol 5

Frilled Lizard, Vol 39

Blue and Gold Macaw, Vol 13

Poison Dart Frogs, Vol 50

Blue Tarantula, Vol 115

African Elephants, Vol 8

Amur Leopard, Vol 89

Sabre Tooth Tiger, Vol 167

Baboon, Vol 174

Sign Up for New Release Emails Here

LisaStrattin.com/subscribe-here

Contents

INTRODUCTION

Labrador Retrievers are a well-balanced, friendly and versatile breed, adaptable to a wide range of functions as well as making very good pets. As a rule they are not excessively prone to being territorial, insecure, aggressive, destructive, hypersensitive, or other difficult traits which sometimes manifest in a variety of breeds, and as the name suggests, they are excellent retrievers.

CHARACTERISTICS

They instinctively enjoy holding objects and even hands or arms in their mouths, which they can do with great gentleness. A Labrador Retriever can carry an egg in its mouth without breaking it!

They are also known to have a very soft feel to their mouth, as a result of being bred to retrieve game such as waterfowl for hunters They are prone to chewing objects (though they can be trained out of this behavior).

APPEARANCE

The most distinguishing characteristics of the Labrador Retriever are its short, dense, weather resistant coat; an "otter" tail; a clean-cut head with broad skull; powerful jaws; and their "kind," friendly eyes, expressive character, intelligence and good temperament.

TEMPERAMENT

Labrador Retrievers have a reputation as a very even-tempered breed and an excellent family dog. This includes getting along well with children of all ages and other animals. Some, particularly those that have continued to be bred specifically for their skills at working in the field (rather than for their appearance), are particularly fast and athletic.

Their fun-loving boisterousness and lack of fear may require training and firm handling at times to ensure it does not get out of hand—an uncontrolled adult can be quite problematic.

Females may be slightly more independent than males.

LIFE SPAN

The Labrador Retriever generally lives to be about 15 years of age.

SIZE

The average adult Labrador Retriever stand about 24 inches tall and weighs around 75 pounds.

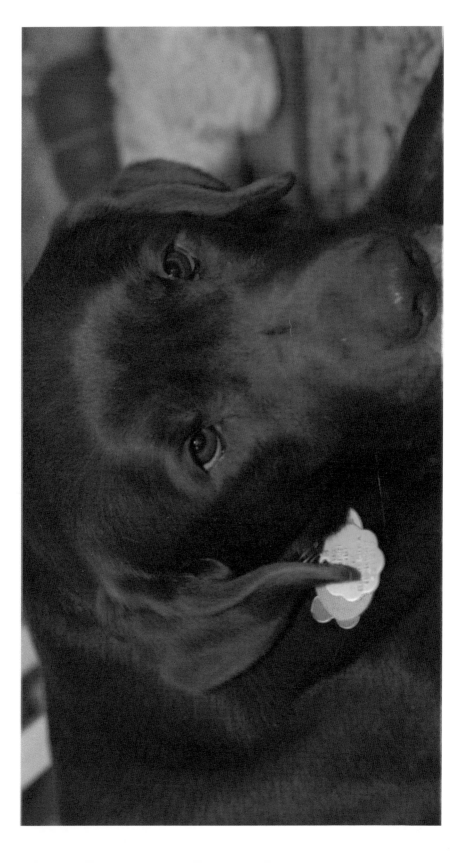

HABITAT

Labrador Retrievers are happy in most homes, whether apartments or houses. They do need regular exercise, so walking yours is a normal responsibility. Visiting a dog park so they can run is also a great way for them to burn off some energy.

DIET

There are many commercially available dog foods that are appropriate for your Labrador Retriever. If you notice any issues, like excessive scratching, you might want to have your veterinarian check to see if your dog has any allergies. If this is determined, your vet can suggest different foods to try for the best health of your dog.

COMMON HEALTH ISSUES

Labradors are somewhat prone to hip and elbow dysplasia, especially larger dogs, though not as much as some other breeds. Labradors also suffer from the risk of knee problems. Be sure to have your dog seen by a veterinarian regularly so that you can quickly address any issues that might arise.

SUITABILITY AS PETS

Labrador Retrievers are great pets. They are loyal and lovable with their human family. If you decide to bring one into your home, you will find that your life is more fun because of this great dog!

COLOR ME

COLOR ME

COLOR ME

COLOR ME

COLOR ME

COLOR ME

COLOR ME

COLOR ME

COLOR ME

Please leave me a review here:

LisaStrattin.com/Review-Vol-279

For more Kindle Downloads Visit Lisa Strattin Author Page on Amazon Author Central

amazon.com/author/lisastrattin

To see upcoming titles, visit my website at LisaStrattin.com– most books available on Kindle!

LisaStrattin.com

FREE BOOK

FOR ALL SUBSCRIBERS – SIGN UP NOW

LisaStrattin.com/Subscribe-Here

LisaStrattin.com/Facebook

LisaStrattin.com/Youtube

Printed in Great Britain
by Amazon

27503154R00025